fashion
sourcebooks

The 1960s

John Peacock

Fashion Sourcebooks The 1960s

With 332 illustrations

Thames and Hudson

For Sandy Richards

British Library Cataloguing-
in-Publication Data
A catalogue record for this book is
available from the British Library.

ISBN 0-500-28040-1

Printed and bound in Slovenia
by Mladinska Knjiga

Contents

The New Look of 1947 which dominated the 1950s was a backward glance at a more 'feminine' time. The 1960s woman, on the other hand, looked firmly ahead. She demanded equal rights and equal pay. She rejected the shackles of voluminous, hampering skirts and the restrictions of corseted waists and high stiletto heels. She wanted to be free, to look young and to have fun.

The way to achieve this young look was obvious: straighten the curves and shorten the skirts. It was a style reminiscent of the 1920s. Skirts began the decade at knee-level and rose steadily, until in 1965 they emerged as the 'mini'. Eventually they shot up above the stocking top, leaving a gap which made the transition to tights inevitable. 'Maxi' skirts made a brief appearance towards the end of the decade, often seen as the skirts of a top coat worn over a 'mini'. And throughout the decade trousers and trouser suits steadily increased in popularity. Styles for evening wear became less rigid – it was not unusual to see both long and short evening dresses at the same function.

The fashion revolution that brought about these developments started in the streets of London, with talented designers like Mary Quant and Barbara Hulanicki. In the United States, James Galanos and Rudi Gernreich were also reaching a young audience. In France, too, some Parisian couturiers – among them Yves Saint Laurent, Pierre Cardin, André Courrèges and Emanuel Ungaro – responded to these new attitudes. In this decade, every one of these creative talents, as well as fashion's leaders and stylesetters, were young. They were lively, highly individual, inventive, gimmicky and greatly concerned with the creation of 'image'.

The main outlets for the new young fashions were small boutiques, selling clothes that were not quite 'one-offs', but were made by individual outworkers producing small quantities in a limited range of colours and sizes. Quant and Hulanicki (of Biba fame) were in the vanguard, but other British and French couturiers began to turn to boutiques and ready-to-wear during the 1960s.

Until the 1960s men's clothes had generally consisted of a traditional three-piece suit of a subtle colour for town wear or a smart tweed sports jacket and toning flannel trousers for country or casual wear (little or no differentiation was made between summer and winter). The details changed almost imperceptibly from season to season or decade to decade. These relatively static styles became less and less acceptable to the 1960s man who was living in a world in which everything seemed to be changing fast and in which pop groups like the Beatles and the Rolling Stones, photographers like David Bailey and Anthony Armstrong-Jones and actors like Michael Caine and Jean-Paul Belmondo exerted a strong sartorial influence.

Boutiques for men sprang up in London's Soho – those in Carnaby Street being the most famous – and Savile Row tailors found that their hegemony was being challenged. Male dress, like female dress, became less class-bound. It also underwent a certain feminization. Men grew their hair long, donned pretty, printed shirts worn open at the neck, discarded neckties, and took to wearing polo-neck sweaters and skintight trousers. By the end of the sixties they were at home in silk, satin and chiffon, as well as frills, bows and lace.

Easy-care synthetic fabrics such as Crimplene, Dacron and Terylene were much used during the 1960s. These materials were crease-resistant, could be permanently pleated, were easy to wash and needed little or no ironing. Synthetic yarns also took dyes easily, giving rise to colours that were clear and bright, reflecting the mood of the period.

Leather-look plastic was also popular and was used for a wide variety of accessories for women, including shoes, knee-high boots, shoulder bags, wrist-length gloves and 'butcher's boy' peaked caps. Plastics were also employed for a range of garments, from brightly coloured mini skirts to see-through raincoats and umbrellas.

In the main, the fashions I have illustrated are such as would have been worn by the middle or upper-middle classes and by people who, while not being 'dedicated followers of fashion', would have had a keen interest in the latest styles.

The sources from which I have drawn – chiefly from Great Britain, North America, France, Italy and Germany – include contemporary magazines, catalogues and journals, original dated photographs, museum collections, and my own costume collection.

This Sourcebook is divided into ten sections, each of which includes four subdivisions covering Day Wear, Evening Wear (alternately, on two occasions, Wedding Wear), Sports and Leisure Wear, and a section on either Underwear and Negligee or Accessories. Following the main illustrations are ten pages of schematic drawings accompanied by detailed notes about each example, giving particulars of colour, cut and trimming as well as other useful information. Then follow two pages of drawings which illustrate the decade 'at a glance' and which demonstrate the evolution of the period and its main development trends.

Biographies of the most important international fashion designers of the decade are also included as well as a list of further reading suggestions into the styles of this period.

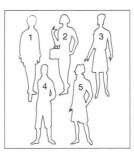
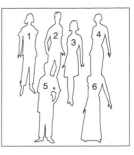

1960 Day Wear

1 Mint-green linen sleeveless dress, bloused bodice above inset waistband, strap opening, large single self-covered button trim, small revers, wide stand-away collar, cut-away armholes, narrow knee-length skirt. Brimless coffee straw hat, self-straw bow trim. Dark-coffee fabric gloves; matching leather shoes, pointed toes, self-leather trim, high stiletto heels. **2** Light-grey flannel two-piece suit: single-breasted jacket, three-button fastening, narrow lapels, flap pockets; straight-cut trousers, no turn-ups. White cotton collar-attached shirt. Red and blue striped silk tie. Grey trilby, wide navy-blue band. Black leather step-in shoes. **3** Cream wool two-piece sleeveless jumper suit: hip-length bloused top, wide round neckline and cut-away armholes bound with navy-blue wool to match flap pockets and hem of knee-length flared skirt. Brimless navy-blue felt hat trimmed with stalk worn on back of head. Short navy-blue leather gloves; matching shoes, pointed toes, self-leather flower trim, high stiletto heels. **4** Beige and tan flecked linen-tweed two-piece suit: long single-breasted jacket fastening with three large burnt-orange leather buttons which match hip-level tie-belt, wide neckline, stand-away collar, three-quarter-length inset sleeves; narrow knee-length skirt. Orange and brown banded straw hat, turned-back brim. Brown leather gloves; matching shoes, pointed toes, fine bar straps, stiletto heels. **5** Brown and black checked double-breasted wool coat, fastening from hip-level inset band to under high black fur collar with large shiny black plastic buttons, three-quarter-length inset sleeves; matching knee-length skirt. Brimless black felt hat, embroidered motif on front. Black suede gloves. Large black patent-leather handbag. Black patent-leather and suede shoes, pointed toes.

Evening Wear

1 Two-piece black wool evening suit: single-breasted jacket, single-button fastening, piped pockets, long roll collar faced with black silk; straight-cut trousers, no turn-ups. Single-breasted red silk waistcoat, scooped collarless neckline; bow-tie in matching fabric. White silk collar-attached shirt, tucked front. Black leather elastic-sided ankle-boots. **2** Silver-grey silk evening ensemble: knee-length sleeveless top, high round neckline edged with silver and crystal beads, semi-fitted bodice and flared skirt cut without waist seam, skirt split on side seams from hem to hip-level; matching tight ankle-length trousers. Silver-grey leather sling-back shoes, spike heels and pointed toecaps in darker silver. **3** Rose-pink, grey and silver patterned silk-satin evening dress, bloused bodice from low waist marked by narrow rose-pink satin belt with bow trim matching wide-set shoulder straps and trim, narrow ankle-length skirt. Full-length pink satin gloves. Silver kid shoes, pointed toes, button trim. **4** Cream silk evening dress, narrow rouleau shoulder straps, vertical pintucks from low neckline of semi-fitted bodice to mid-calf-level of flared skirt, no waist seam, skirt hem finished with wide gathered frill to ground. Elbow-length chocolate-brown fabric gloves; matching shoes. **5** Bottle-green satin evening dress, horizontal panels beaded and embroidered in black, fitted bodice, wide boat-shaped neckline, elbow-length inset sleeves, ankle-length bell-shaped skirt, black satin belt tied into bow on centre-front. Elbow-length black satin gloves; matching shoes.

Sports and Leisure Wear

1 Ski wear. Long pale-blue weatherproof cotton ski-jacket, fur-lined, centre-front zip fastening from band on hem to under fur-lined and trimmed hood, adjustable button straps on sides of hem, long raglan sleeves, two waist-level diagonally-placed piped pockets with zip fastenings, top-stitched edges and detail. Dark-blue stretch-nylon ski-pants tucked into black leather lace-up ankle-boots. Dark-blue leather mittens lined and trimmed with fur. **2** Beach wear. All-in-one cotton jumpsuit with printed patchwork pattern in greens and yellows, concealed centre-front zip fastening to under high round neckline, shaped cut-away armholes, bodice and trousers cut without waist seam, narrow legs, small split on each seam above hem. Outsized beach bag in matching fabric. **3** Holiday wear. Natural colour linen dress, wide shoulder straps buttoned onto straight neckline of hip-length bloused bodice, knee-length flared skirt. Beige canvas shoes, green leather trim, pointed toes. **4** Country wear. Olive-green knitted-wool sweater, wide V-shaped neckline, long inset sleeves, turned-back ribbed cuffs. Dark-cream brushed-cotton collar-attached shirt, collar worn open. Olive-green and red spotted silk cravat. Dark-brown cotton cord breeches, side pockets, narrow legs. Handknitted rust-brown stockings. Dark-brown leather lace-up brogues. **5** Country wear. Tan knitted-wool sweater, outsized ribbed polo collar, three-quarter-length sleeves set into large square armholes, ribbed hems. Knee-length tan, green and cream checked wool culottes, side hip pockets. Tan knitted-wool tights. Brown leather lace-up ankle-boots, pointed toes, flat heels.

Underwear and Negligee

1 Fine pale-yellow cotton pyjamas patterned with multicoloured posies of flowers: hip-length top, high round neckline, edges of peter-pan collar bound in plain yellow cotton, rouleau bow trim matching piped off-the-shoulder yoke seam and hems of puff sleeves, hem curved up to side seams, bow trim matching hems of narrow mid-calf-length trousers. Yellow velvet slippers, pointed toes, flower trim, flat heels. **2** Peach-pink brassiere, boned support between fitted cups, lace trim and edging, elasticated side panels, back fastening, adjustable shoulder straps. Peach-pink elasticated cotton girdle, double fabric front panel, lace-effect side front panels, adjustable suspenders. Flesh-coloured nylon stockings. **3** Combined cream cotton strapless brassiere and hip-length girdle, shaped and fitted cups, lace trim and edging, wired supports, back fastening, adjustable suspenders. Primrose-yellow nylon waist slip, nylon lace edging. Cream satin slippers. **4** White cotton brassiere, elasticated panel between seamed cups, narrow halter straps. White stretch-nylon pantie-girdle, wide waistband, shaped front panel, long legs, zigzag stitched detail. **5** White cotton pyjama suit spotted with dark-green: wraporer collarless jacket, edges bound in dark-green to match tie-belt, elbow-length kimono sleeves; straight-cut trousers. **6** Pale-coffee nylon nightdress, shaped shoulder straps and upper part of bodice cut in one and edged with cream nylon lace matching hem of floor-length skirt, gathered from shaped waist seam. Coffee slippers with pointed toes.

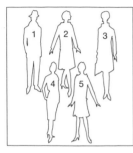

1961 Day Wear

1 Short camel-coloured wool car coat, double-breasted fastening with leather buttons, wide lapels, large collar, hip-level patch-and-flap pockets, top-stitched edges and detail. Dark-brown knitted-wool polo-neck sweater. Tapered beige wool trousers, no turn-ups. Beige brushed-felt trilby. Elastic-sided brown leather ankle-boots. **2** Sage-green, lilac and grey wool-tweed two-piece suit: hip-length unfitted jacket, double-breasted fastening, narrow lapels, stand-away collar, vertical welt pockets set into side panel seams at hip-level, full-length inset sleeves; knee-length box-pleated skirt. Sage-green patent-leather shoes, pointed toes, bow trim, high stiletto heels. **3** Cream and pink flecked wool-tweed coat, flared knee-length skirts from high waist position, double-breasted fastening with large cream wool buttons from mid-thigh to under stand collar, full-length inset sleeves, top stitched edges and detail. Deep-pink brimless felt hat. Black leather gloves; matching outsized handbag and shoes with pointed toes. **4** Smoke-blue slubbed-linen dress, semi-bloused bodice above wide inset waistband, dark-blue leather double-breasted button trim from waist to low hip-level, wide square neckline, short inset sleeves, straight knee-length skirt, pockets in side panel seams. Cream leather shoes, navy-blue leather pointed toecaps and high stiletto heels. **5** Light-grey flannel dress, hip-length semi-fitted bodice, wide boat-shaped neckline trimmed in dark-grey to match hip-belt, cuffs of elbow-length inset sleeves and lining of pleats in knee-length flared skirt; neckline and hip-belt have matching buckle detail. Black leather shoes, pointed toes, medium-high stiletto heels.

Evening Wear

1 Fine silk-satin evening dress patterned with outsized flowers in greens and blues on pearl-grey background, boned fitted bodice, cross-over draped panels form small train from waist-level at back, narrow self-fabric rouleau shoulder straps, straight ankle-length skirt, split on one side from hem to knee-level. Full-length emerald-green satin gloves; matching shoes with pointed toes. **2** Pale-dusty-pink silk-taffeta cocktail dress, semi-fitted bodice cut in one piece with knee-length flared skirt, square neckline, wide shoulder straps, outsized self-fabric bow on centre-front at hip-level, centre of bow trimmed with self-fabric roses and leaves. Silver kid sling-back shoes, pointed toes, high stiletto heels. **3** Navy-blue silk cocktail dress, bloused bodice pleated from wide round neckline, pleats lined with rose-pink satin matching cowl at back, wide self-fabric pleated cummerbund, large bow decoration on one side, brooch trim, straight knee-length skirt. Elbow-length navy-blue satin gloves; matching shoes, pointed toes, fine straps, high stiletto heels. **4** Two-piece black wool evening suit: double-breasted jacket, wide lapels faced in black satin matching covered buttons, piped pockets; tapered trousers, outside seams trimmed with satin braid, no turn-ups. Black kid-leather lace-up shoes. **5** Green-grey lightweight wool-crepe evening dress, sleeveless bloused bodice from hip-level, high round neckline edged with detachable feather collar, straight ankle-length skirt, split from hem to knee-level on one side, lined with green satin. Green satin shoes, pointed toes, crossed bar straps.

Sports and Leisure Wear

1 Winter sports wear. Orange and brown heavyweight wool-tweed poncho, pointed hemline edged with dark-orange wool tasselled fringe, drawstring hood, dark-orange wool pom-pon trim. Tight brown heavyweight stretch-nylon ski-pants worn tucked into lace-up brown leather après-ski ankle-boots, pointed toes, flat heels. **2** Swimwear. Royal-blue sailcloth swimming shorts, wide legs split on outside seams above hem, elasticated waistband. **3** Swimwear. Powder-blue acetate and cotton mixture stretch-fabric swimsuit, pleated reinforced central panel, self-fabric bow trim under shaped and boned cups, narrow shoulder straps, short skirt, built-in briefs. **4** Beachwear. Hip-length white knitted-cotton T-shirt, short cap sleeves edged in navy-blue to match deep V-shaped neckline, bow trim, infill and fitted shorts with high-cut legs. Navy-blue leather thong mules. **5** Tennis. Cream and white striped cotton dress, vertical stripes used on hip-length semi-fitted bodice, cut-away armholes, straight neckline, centre-front nick above seam running through to hem of knee-length bias-cut skirt, hip-level bow-tied belt, horizontal stripes. White cotton ankle socks. White canvas lace-up sports shoes.

Accessories

1 Olive-green leather handbag, thick rouleau handle, clasp fastening. **2** Green leather shoes, pointed toes, button trim, stiletto heels. **3** Fine cream straw cloche hat, wide orange band, bow trim. **4** Tan leather sandals, strap-and-buckle fastening, crepe soles. **5** Cream leather lace-up shoes, top-stitched brown leather fronts. **6** Navy-blue leather shoes, pointed toes, bow trim, stiletto heels. **7** Brimless fur hat, pom-pon trim. **8** Black leather step-in shoes, strap detail. **9** Black leather shoes, strap-and-buckle fastening. **10** Cream leather shoes, black leather trim, stiletto heels. **11** Elastic-sided black leather boots, pointed toes, stacked heels. **12** Elastic-sided black leather ankle-boots, pointed toes, low stacked heels. **13** Red leather pumps, navy-blue bow and trim, flat heels. **14** Beige suede lace-up ankle-boots, crepe soles. **15** Grey patent-leather shoes, square toes, buttoned-strap trim. **16** Red leather shoes, pointed toes, threaded-bow trim. **17** White leather shoes, black toecaps and bow trim. **18** Bottle-green straw cloche hat, wide pink band, white flower trim. **19** Lilac satin gloves, ruched sides, button trim. **20** Tan leather gauntlet gloves, bow trim. **21** Red-and-white patterned hat, black band and rosette trim. **22** Brown leather handbag, flap, stud fastening, thick handle. **23** Crocheted cotton hat. **24** Sage-green canvas bag, tan leather buckled straps, long handle. **25** Black evening bag, sequin trim. **26** Brown leather handbag, clasp fastening, double handles. **27** Brown leather shoes, pointed toes, narrow bar straps. **28** Black leather shoes, wrapover strap, button trim. **29** Black leather shoes, black suede frill. **30** Navy-blue leather shoes, narrow diagonal straps, button trim. **31** Tan leather handbag, mock-flap with straps, thick handle. **32** Black cotton gloves, ruched pleat, button trim.

   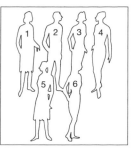

1962 Day Wear

1 Pink wool-tweed two-piece suit: semi-fitted waist-length jacket, single-breasted fastening with four buttons, high round neckline, padded binding and rouleau bow tie, bracelet-length inset sleeves, turned-back cuffs; knee-length flared skirt, wide centre-front box-pleat. Beige felt hat, split brim turned up at back forming peak at front. Brown leather gloves; matching handbag and shoes, pointed toes, stiletto heels. 2 Black and pink checked wool-tweed two-piece suit: short edge-to-edge box-shaped jacket, stand collar bound in black to match hems of long inset sleeves, buttoned patch pockets and front edges; knee-length flared skirt. Semi-fitted pink silk blouse, high round neckline, long cuffed sleeves. Black patent-leather T-strap shoes, low heels. 3 Cream and beige wool-tweed coat, single-breasted fastening with three black leather buttons, three-quarter-length raglan-style sleeves, wide stand collar, hip-level welt pockets, skirts tapered to knee-length hem. Black leather gloves; matching handbag and sling-back shoes, pointed toes, side bow trim, stiletto heels. 4 Sage-green flecked linen-tweed dress, sleeveless hip-length semi-fitted bodice, armholes bound in black to match binding on high round neckline, bow tie and inset band on hipline, knee-length flared skirt, self-fabric inset godet on each side centre-front and back. Black leather shoes, pointed toes, bar-strap and bow trim, stiletto heels. 5 Cream showerproof cotton raincoat, double-breasted fastening, raglan sleeves, strap-and-buckle trim matching shoulder trim, floating yoke, welt pockets, knee-length skirts, buckled belt, top-stitched edges and detail. Tapered brown wool trousers. Cream collar-attached shirt. Narrow brown wool tie. Elastic-sided brown leather ankle-boots.

Evening Wear

1 Navy-blue wool and mohair mixture two-piece evening suit: single-breasted jacket, single-button fastening, long shawl collar faced in navy-blue satin matching split-sleeve cuffs, covered buttons and under-collar bow tie; tapered trousers, no turn-ups. White cotton collar-attached shirt, concealed fastening under box-pleat. Black leather lace-up shoes. 2 Silver-grey satin evening dress, high round neckline, sleeveless semi-fitted bodice embroidered with silver, pink and crystal beads and bead fringing, full-length skirt gathered under pink satin ribbon belt, bow tie on centre-front. Full-length pink satin gloves; matching shoes with pointed toes, fine bow trim. 3 Fine pale-orange silk-chiffon evening dress printed with outsized paisley pattern in pinks, yellows and browns, bloused bodice above gold kid buckled belt, low pointed neckline, small stand-away collar, short inset sleeves, ankle-length gathered skirt; deep-orange silk underdress, strapless and boned bodice, ankle-length flared skirt. Dark-cream fabric gloves. Gold kid shoes, pointed toes, medium-high stiletto heels. 4 Black wool-crepe evening dress, slashed neckline, hip-length semi-fitted bodice, full-length inset sleeves, deep band of bead embroidery at wrist-level matching detail on hipline and above hem on straight ankle-length skirt. Black satin shoes, pointed toes. 5 Rich cream satin evening dress patterned with lilac and blue flowers and gold leaves, strapless boned bodice cut in one with straight ankle-length skirt, neckline edged with pleated plain gold satin, bow trim on one side, matching gold fabric forms wide box-pleat in back of skirt. Cream satin shoes, pointed toes, fine bar-strap and bow trim.

Sports and Leisure Wear

1 Beach wear. Orange, red and green floral cotton bikini: bra top, separated and wired pre-formed cups, halter straps, back fastening; briefs with elasticated waist, high-cut legs. 2 Beach wear. Two-piece beach suit: pale-green cotton shirt, brown and green striped cotton collar matching cuffs of long inset sleeves, trim on two chest-level patch pockets and shorts with elasticated waistband. Light-brown leather sandals, open sides and toes, detachable back straps. 3 Country wear. Sage-green and beige wool-tweed two-piece suit: short single-breasted jacket, three-button stepped fastening from waist-level to under long pointed collar, three-quarter-length inset sleeves, turned-back cuffs, waist-level patch pockets with pleat trim and buttoned flaps; knee-length flared skirt. Sage-green knitted-wool polo-neck sweater. Brimless red fox-fur hat. Dark-cream knitted-wool tights. Long brown leather boots, side-zip fastening, pointed toes, low spike heels. 4 Casual/Spectator sports wear. Waist-length red leather sleeveless tunic, wide boat-shaped neckline, side-zip fastening. White cotton collar-attached shirt, full-length sleeves, deep cuffs, four-button fastening. Knee-length black and white checked wool breeches; matching butcher's boy peaked cap. Red knitted-wool tights. Black leather lace-up shoes, pointed toes, low heels. 5 Tennis. Short white cotton dress, wide round neckline and deep armholes bound in self-fabric, hip-length semi-fitted bodice, box-pleated skirt. Elastic-sided white canvas shoes, low rubber wedge heels.

Underwear and Negligee

1 Pastel-blue nylon knee-length sleeveless nightdress, low square neckline and armholes edged in fine nylon lace, base of yoke edged with scalloped lace to match hem of gathered skirt. 2 White knitted-cotton singlet, low scooped neckline and cut-away armholes; briefs in matching fabric, double-fabric front panel, high-cut legs, elasticated waist. 3 Black lace bra mounted over stiffened flesh-coloured satin, seamed and wired cups, black satin shoulder straps set wide apart continue under cups, fine lace trim, back fastening. Elasticated black satin pantie-girdle, black lace panels over flesh-coloured satin each side centre-front, fine lace trim on waist and around high-cut legs. 4 White cotton bra, deep plunging neckline, seamed cups lined with fine pre-formed foam, elasticated side panels, adjustable shoulder straps, back fastening. Elasticated white cotton girdle, cross-over top-stitched panels front and back, four adjustable and detachable suspenders. 5 Pale-turquoise nylon slip, bra-top edged and trimmed with black nylon lace to match hem of knee-length flared skirt, adjustable shoulder straps. 6 Dull-peach-pink stretch-cotton-satin bra, low-cut neckline, elasticated panel between seamed cups over pre-formed foam, embroidered trim, elasticated shoulder straps, back fastening. Pink stretch-nylon-satin pantihose, double-fabric front panel, embroidered trim, long legs, scalloped hems with bow trim matching detail on waist.

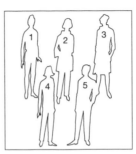

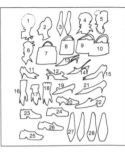

1963 Day Wear

1 Poppy-red linen two-piece suit: hip-length semi-fitted jacket, single-breasted fastening with outsized pearl buttons from above hem to under low round neckline, curved yoke seam, short dolman sleeves; knee-length box-pleated skirt. White silk scarf draped over head and shoulders. Short white cotton gloves. Red leather shoes, fine rouleau straps, pointed toes, high stiletto heels. **2** Powder-blue fine wool-tweed two-piece jumper suit: semi-fitted hip-length top, buttoned flap pockets set into seam above hipline, button fastening under high collar, dropped shoulderline, long inset sleeves, top-stitched edges and detail; knee-length straight skirt. Short coffee leather gloves; matching shoes, chisel toes, high stiletto heels. **3** Rust-brown cotton-corduroy single-breasted jacket, single-button fastening, large patch-and-flap pockets, chest-level flap pocket. Tapered dark-brown wool trousers, no turn-ups. Pale-grey cotton shirt, attached white cotton collar. Grey, brown and red striped knitted-silk tie. Tan leather step-in shoes. **4** Three-quarter-length white wool coat, double-breasted fastening from waist to under stand-away collar, three-quarter-length inset sleeves, hip-level diagonal welt pockets. Knee-length black and white checked wool skirt. Long white fabric gloves. Black leather shoes, pointed toes, high stiletto heels. **5** Grey wool-flannel dress striped in navy-blue and red, semi-fitted bodice and knee-length straight skirt cut without waist seam, self-fabric tie-belt on hipline, strap fastening from above hemline to under narrow revers, long pointed collar, full-length inset sleeves, buttoned cuffs, low hip-level patch pockets, button trim. Red leather shoes, pointed toes, narrow bar straps, stiletto heels.

Evening Wear

1 Formal evening dress, black ribbon-lace fitted bodice, wide scalloped neckline matching short sleeves and hem, full-length oyster-cream satin flared skirt, large self-fabric bow trim on centre-front at hip-level above unpressed knife-pleat. Full-length black satin gloves; matching shoes with pointed toes. **2** Jade-green silk cocktail dress, deep cut-away armholes, low V-shaped neckline, self-fabric bow at base, brooch trim, knee-length skirt flares from seam under bust. Jade-green satin shoes, pointed toes, high stiletto heels. **3** White linen single-breasted tuxedo jacket, single-button fastening, long shawl collar faced with white silk, matching covered buttons, hip-level piped pockets. Tapered black linen trousers, black silk ribbon stripe on outside seams, no turn-ups. White cotton collar-attached shirt, concealed fastening. Black satin bow-tie. Black leather shoes. **4** Evening dress, sleeveless brown silk bloused bodice embroidered all over with transparent shiny sequins, low scooped neckline, cut-away armholes form wide shoulder straps, brown velvet ribbon bow trim on centre-front under bust, floor-length flared skirt. Full-length brown suede gloves; matching shoes, pointed toes, delicate crossed-strap trim. **5** Dusty-pink silk-crepe evening dress, fitted bodice from under bust seam, wide self-fabric shoulder straps tied into flat bows on top of shoulders, narrow ankle-length skirt, gathers under bust seam. Large unlined self-fabric stole edged with bright-pink feathers. Pink satin shoes, pointed toes, high stiletto heels.

Sports and Leisure Wear

1 Beach wear. Lime-green cotton-jersey one-piece bathing costume, bloused bodice from above self-fabric belt, bow trim, shaped neckline, narrow shoulder straps, self-fabric briefs. Burnt-orange draped cotton-towelling hat. Gold kid-leather thong mules, leaf-shaped straps. **2** Casual wear. Red and yellow flecked wool-tweed two-piece jumper suit: long unfitted top, full-length flared inset sleeves, wide neckline, red knitted-wool deep polo-neck collar matching tie-belt and hip-level pockets; trousers tapered to narrow hems. Red leather shoes, blunt toes, tongues, button trim. **3** Golf. Dark-brown leather sleeveless jerkin top, low V-shaped neckline, welt pockets set into hip-level seam, hand top-stitched edges and detail. Red, orange, brown and grey striped knitted-wool sweater, wide neckline, stand-away polo-neck collar, three-quarter-length sleeves. Dark-grey wool flared knee-length skirt, inverted box-pleats each side centre-front. Dark-brown leather peaked cap. Brown leather lace-up shoes, fringed tongues, round toes, flat heels. **4** Casual wear. Pale-yellow knitted-wool cardigan-jacket, single-breasted fastening, self-colour rib matching hems of long inset sleeves and pointed collar, multicoloured embroidered flower sprays under shoulder and above waist. Silver-grey wool-flannel tapered trousers. Bright-yellow ankle socks. Mid-grey suede step-in shoes, fringed strap-and-button trim, square toes, flat heels. **5** Casual wear. Mid-grey, dark-grey and red striped knitted-cotton shirt, loop and button under collar, plain red cotton strap with single-button fastening matches hip-level welt pockets and buttoned cuffs of long inset sleeves. Tapered mid-grey cotton trousers, narrow hems, no turn-ups, side hip pockets. Black leather lace-up shoes, round toes, top-stitched detail.

Accessories

1 Brimless red and brown fur hat. **2** Red wool beret, top-stitched band, gathers at front. **3** Gunmetal-grey leather shoes, pointed toes, bow trim. **4** Red leather peaked cap. **5** Navy-blue wool beret, red wool pom-pon trim. **6** Bottle-green felt pillbox hat, self-fabric bow trim. **7** Sage-green leather handbag, double handles, clasp fastening. **8** Grey leather handbag, flat handle, large flap, stud fastening. **9** Black leather handbag, single handle, clasp fastening, top-stitched trim. **10** Red leather handbag, gilt clasp and trim, threaded double rouleau handles. **11** Black leather shoes, pointed toes, black suede straps, gilt bow trim, stiletto heels. **12** Black patent-leather sling-back shoes, pointed toes, black petersham ribbon bow trim. **13** Navy-blue leather sling-back shoes, pointed toes, red leather straps and trim, stiletto heels. **14** Black leather sling-back shoes, red leather straps and trim. **15** Black patent-leather shoes, open sides, self-bow trim, stiletto heels. **16** Long black leather gloves, button trim. **17** Short grey fabric gloves, turned-down cuffs, gilt stud trim. **18** Pink suede gloves, scalloped edges. **19** Navy-blue leather shoes, open sides, self-bow trim, cream side panels, perforated decoration. **20** Beige suede shoes, round toes, perforated decoration. **21** Dark-green pearlized-leather shoes, pointed toes, open sides. **22** Light-brown leather step-in shoes, strap-and-button trim, low stacked heels. **23** Black leather shoes, strap-and-buckle fastening, square toes. **24** Brown elastic-sided step-in shoes. **25** Black leather elastic-sided step-in shoes. **26** Light-brown leather moccasin-style shoes, self-leather trim. **27** Black leather lace-up shoes, pointed toes. **28** Dark-green leather shoes, round toes, self-leather trim.

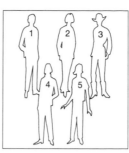

1964 Day Wear

1 Navy-blue rayon dress, semi-fitted bodice and above-knee-length flared skirt cut without waist seam, wide neckline, white rayon peter-pan collar, cut-away armholes. White straw hat, turned-back brim. White nylon tights spotted in navy-blue. Navy-blue leather shoes, pointed toes, low spike heels. 2 Cherry-red linen and rayon mixture two-piece jumper suit: waist-length unfitted top, deep scooped neckline, wide self-fabric binding, buttoned cross-over on centre-front infilled with pale-blue and white patterned fabric, button fastening, collar set onto wide neckline, short self-fabric inset sleeves, machined hems; above-knee-length straight skirt, gathers at waist. Short dark-blue leather gloves; matching clutch bag and shoes, pointed toes, low heels. 3 Grey and white slubbed-silk jacket, single-breasted fastening, narrow lapels, diagonal flap pockets. Fine black wool tapered trousers, no turn-ups. Pale-grey cotton collar-attached shirt, button-down collar points, red knitted-silk tie. Black leather elastic-sided step-in shoes, square toes. 4 Brown cotton-corduroy dress, semi-fitted bodice and above-knee-length skirt cut without waist seam, deep scooped neckline infilled with detachable cream knitted-cotton polo neck matching cuffs on hems of three-quarter-length inset sleeves. Brown leather shoes, almond-shaped toes, keyhole, bow trim, low thick heels. 5 Black wool two-piece suit: edge-to-edge unfitted jacket, lapels faced in pink silk to match lining and hip-length blouse, low V-shaped neckline, self-silk ties, long sleeves with tied cuffs show under full-length inset sleeves of jacket; above-knee-length flared skirt. Black leather bar-strap shoes, square toes, low thick heels.

Wedding Wear

1 Cream silk-dupion wedding dress, sleeveless fitted bodice, scooped neckline, small split above centre-front seam, cut-away armholes, self-fabric belt tied into large bow at front, ground-length flared skirt, three deep tucks above hemline. Cream silk-net veil attached to silk rose headdress. Cream silk shoes, pointed toes. 2 Pale-coffee silk wedding dress, fitted bodice, horizontal tucks from waist to under scalloped edge of off-the-shoulder elbow-length coffee lace collar, tight full-length sleeves, ankle-length bell-shaped skirt, three tucks above hemline. Long pale-coffee net veil, velvet ribbon bow headdress. Coffee satin shoes, almond-shaped toes, low heels. 3 Dark-grey wool tailcoat, single-button fastening. Single-breasted pale-grey wool waistcoat. Grey and black striped wool tapered trousers, no turn-ups. White shirt, wing collar. Grey, white and black striped silk cravat. Light-grey top hat. Grey fabric gloves. Black leather lace-up shoes, square toes. 4 White cotton-organza wedding dress, fitted bodice, deep inset band from waist to under bust trimmed with band of white cotton flower-shaped braid matching slashed neckline, hems of tight full-length inset sleeves and trim at hip-level and knee-level on ground-length gathered skirt, tucks over hem of organza overskirt, bodice and skirt mounted over plain white cotton. White silk water-lily headdress, short white cotton-net veil. White kid shoes, pointed toes. 5 White silk wedding dress, semi-fitted bodice and ankle-length flared skirt cut in one piece without waist seam, round neckline, three-quarter-length flared inset sleeves edged with shaped stiffened bands, matching hemline. Long white silk-tulle veil attached to white silk headband. White kid shoes, pointed toes, stiletto heels.

Sports and Leisure Wear

1 Golf. Grey knitted-wool cardigan-jacket, single-breasted fastening with black leather ball buttons, high round neckline, front edges and hem bound in black leather to match cuffs of inset sleeves and hip-level welt pockets. Tapered grey wool trousers, no turn-ups. Black knitted-wool polo-neck sweater. Black leather shoes, fringed tongues, square toecaps. 2 Country wear. Brown and tan wool-tweed two-piece suit: double-breasted jacket, high fastening under narrow lapels, small collar, side panel seams, hip-level flap pockets, full-length inset sleeves; tapered trousers. Handknitted brown wool polo-neck sweater. Brown leather shoes, keyhole front, bow fastening. 3 Riding. Blue brushed-cotton shirt, small collar and revers, high yoke seam, patch pockets with box-pleat and buttoned flap, full-length inset sleeves, buttoned cuffs. Tight beige cotton trousers, deep waistband, brown leather buckled belt. High brown leather boots, top-stitched trim, square toes, low stacked heels. 4 Tenpin bowling. Dark-yellow handknitted wool collarless cardigan-jacket, single-breasted fastening with grey leather buttons matching piping on high round neckline, front edges, hems and trim on full-length inset sleeves and hip-level patch pockets. Tapered dark-yellow wool trousers. Red knitted-wool polo-neck sweater. Red cotton socks. Red leather step-in shoes, high tongues, strap trim, square toes, flat heels. 5 Holiday wear. Blue and white striped knitted-cotton T-shirt, slashed neckline, short inset sleeves. Red cotton-corduroy tapered trousers, narrow hems, stirrups under feet. Red leather pumps, pointed toes, flat heels.

Underwear and Negligee

1 Flesh-coloured Lycra one-piece footless body suit, low scooped neckline, narrow shoulder straps, low-cut armholes. 2 One-piece white cotton longline girdle and bra patterned with tiny blue and green flowers, narrow shoulder straps cut in one with underwired and seamed cups, fine lace edging matching side panel seams, centre-front zip fastening, four adjustable and detachable suspenders. Flesh-coloured nylon stockings. 3 Pink-cream silk-velvet housecoat, three-quarter-length sleeves and ankle-length skirt gathered from round cream satin shoulder yoke, wide round neckline, deep-pink piping matching edges of short opening, small covered buttons and bound hems of sleeves, skirt and sleeve hems decorated with scattered appliqué of pink and cream satin leaf shapes. 4 Black machine-knitted Courtelle and wool mixture two-piece set patterned with posies of pink flowers: fitted top, low scooped neckline, fine black lace edging matching scooped armholes and elasticated waist and hems of longline knickers. 5 Black nylon-satin bra, low neckline, wide shoulder straps, seamed and underwired cups, edged with black nylon lace, back fastening. Black Lycra pull-on pantie-girdle, draped cross-over front panels from side-front panel seams, short legs.

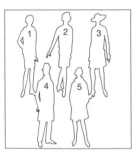

1965 Day Wear

1 Grey and brown wool-tweed two-piece suit: unfitted hip-length jacket, double-breasted wrapover front, strap-and-buckle fastening, wide pointed lapels, stand-away collar, curved top-stitched seam from under arm, matching pockets, full-length inset sleeves, top-stitched edges and detail; straight mini-skirt two or three inches above knee. Black polo-neck sweater. Black tights. Black leather step-in shoes, high tongues, round toes, low heels. **2** Hip-length unfitted cream wool top, high round neckline, full-length inset sleeves, black patent-leather belt on low waistline. Straight black wool mini-skirt. Black patent-leather shoes, almond-shaped toes, low thick heels. **3** Berry-red Terylene and wool mixture tweed dress, hip-length sleeveless bodice, top-stitched bib panel matching wide neckline, deep armholes and hip-level buttoned belt, flared mini-skirt, side-front box-pleats. Red felt hat, small crown, deep ribbon band, wide brim. Short black leather gloves; matching shoes, high vamp, button trim, low thick heels. **4** Grey and black striped wool-tweed double-breasted knee-length overcoat, black fur collar, breast pocket, hip-level welt pockets. Tapered grey wool trousers, no turn-ups. Grey trilby, wide ribbon band, narrow brim. Black leather gloves and lace-up shoes. **5** Egg-yellow wool coat, single-breasted stepped fastening with brass buttons, high collar, full-length inset sleeves, hip-level flap pockets, flared skirts two or three inches above knee. Shiny blue plastic bar-strap shoes, round toes, flat heels.

Evening Wear

1 Black lace evening dress, fitted bodice and ankle-length flared skirt cut without waist seam, low scooped neckline, scalloped edge matching edges of three-quarter-length inset sleeves and hem of skirt; underbodice and underskirt of same shape in black silk. Black satin shoes, pointed toes, stiletto heels. **2** Black silk-chiffon cocktail-evening dress, high neckline, bloused bodice above black satin belt tied into bow at front, matching black satin bindings of three-quarter-length dolman sleeves and hems of two-tier pleated mini-skirt; strapless black silk-crepe underbodice and flared underskirt. Black satin shoes, almond-shaped toes, satin bow and rose trim, low thick heels. **3** White Terylene-crepe evening dress, semi-fitted bodice and flared ankle-length skirt cut without waist seam, slashed neckline, bust-length yoke banded with blue, green and silver sequins to match cuffs of full-length bishop-style inset sleeves and hemline of skirt. Silver kid shoes, round toes. **4** Red silk mini-length semi-fitted theatre coat embroidered all over with large red sequins, single-breasted fastening with large covered buttons which match wide silk binding of front edges, round neckline and hems of three-quarter-length flared inset sleeves. Brimless cap in matching sequined fabric. Red leather sling-back shoes, pointed toes, low thick heels. **5** White and gold brocade evening dress, semi-fitted bodice and straight ankle-length skirt cut without waist seam, skirt split from hemline to knee-level on one side, deep V-shaped neckline, cut-away armholes, low back. Gold kid shoes, almond-shaped toes, self-kid rose on one side, low louis heels.

Sports and Leisure Wear

1 Ski wear. Royal-blue quilted-nylon sleeveless ski jacket, zip fastening from hem to under rounded stand collar, inset waistband with small quilting to match hip-level diagonal welt pockets. Black knitted-wool fine rib polo-neck sweater. Black brushed-nylon ski-pants. Royal-blue leather gauntlets. Black leather ski-boots. **2** Holiday wear. Yellow cotton dress, hip-length sleeveless bloused bodice, inserted graded sunburst bands of bright-red cotton from low round bound neckline, matching flared mini-skirt and hip-level tie-belt. Red leather shoes, almond-shaped toes, decorative side straps, bow trim, low thick heels. **3** Casual wear. Pale turquoise and silver-grey knitted-wool skinny-rib sweater, fitted body ribbed from low round neckline to hem, matching elbow-length sleeves. Dark-turquoise wool mini-skirt, flared shaped panels from V-shaped hip yoke, top-stitched detail, tan leather belt, oval metal buckle. Tan leather bar-strap shoes, side-buckle fastening, almond-shaped toes. **4** Casual wear. Short navy-blue wool coat, double-breasted fastening under wide-set collar, full-length inset sleeves, strap-and-button trim above hem, hip-level diagonal pockets, top-stitched edges. Yellow, navy-blue and cream checked wool tapered trousers. Navy-blue and yellow patterned silk scarf. Navy-blue peaked cap. Navy-blue leather step-in shoes, chain trim, round toes, flat heels. **5** Surfing wear. White knitted-cotton T-shirt, wide neckline edged in bright-green to match hem of shirt and hems of short inset sleeves, bright-green and yellow logo on chest. Bright-green cotton-sailcloth shorts, white-trimmed edges and seams.

Accessories

1 Black leather peaked cap. **2** Natural-straw trilby, twisted ribbon band, narrow brim. **3** Red felt hat, large crown, flat top, wide brim, flat edge. **4** Cream straw hat, wide brim, flat edge, brown ribbon trim, centre-front bow. **5** Brown leather trilby, seamed panel front and back, inset band, narrow brim. **6** Beige suede lace-up shoes, man-made soles. **7** Dark-plum suede shoes, wide bar straps, square toes, low thick heels. **8** Brimless white felt hat, black feather and brooch trim. **9** Dark-green leather sandals, strap-and-buckle fastening, open sides, openwork detail, crepe soles. **10** Cream leather shoes, brown leather bar straps, heels and trim. **11** Brimless grey felt hat. **12** Cream dull-plastic shoes, threaded straps through high tongues, wedge heels. **13** Brown leather step-in shoes, strap-and-button trim, flat heels. **14** Navy-blue felt trilby, narrow curled brim. **15** Black leather bar-strap shoes, button fastening, almond-shaped toes, high thick heels. **16** Black patent-leather shoes, large self-patent buckle trimmed with black grosgrain, medium-thick heel. **17** Sage-green felt trilby, black petersham band and bow, matching trim on narrow curled brim. **18** Bright-green plastic T-strap sling-back sandals, peep toes, low thick heels. **19** Black leather sling-back shoes, white strap and trim, low heels. **20** Tan leather driving gloves, elasticated strap over large keyhole opening. **21** Olive-green leather driving gloves, large and small perforated decoration. **22** Brown leather handbag, metal clasp and trim, thick rouleau handle, top-stitched detail. **23** Navy-blue leather handbag, flap, metal clasp fastening, thick rouleau handle. **24** Dark-brown leather boots, matching narrow buckled strap under top edge of cream leather uppers, flat heels.

1966 Day Wear

1 Silver plastic raincoat spotted in red, double-breasted fastening, wide pointed lapels and collar, full-length inset sleeves, buckled self-fabric belt and covered buttons, hip-level diagonal welt pockets, flared mini-length skirts. Square pillbox hat in matching fabric. Red leather shoes, round toes, high tongues, low thick heels. 2 Navy-blue and white striped knitted-cotton dress, hip-length unfitted bodice, wide neckline bound in plain red knitted-cotton to match deep cuffs of long inset sleeves and bound hem of gathered mini-skirt. Red cotton-sailcloth butcher's boy peaked cap. Red leather shoes, almond-shaped toes, wide bar straps. 3 Green, cream and tan striped fine wool jumper suit: hip-length unfitted top, single-breasted fastening under small collar, full-length shirt sleeves, deep cuffs, buttoned hipband, top-stitched edges and detail; straight mini-skirt. Dark-cream wool tights. Shiny tan plastic shoes, large buckle trim, square toes, low thick heels. 4 Light-brown wool jacket, high three-button fastening under narrow lapels, small collar, three flap pockets. Dark-brown cotton-jumbo-cord tapered trousers, no turn-ups. White collar-attached shirt, small collar with round edges. Red and brown spotted silk tie. Brown leather elastic-sided ankle-boots, square toes. 5 Grey-pink Crimplene-jersey dress, hip-length unfitted sleeveless bodice, double-breasted jacket-effect with self-fabric covered buttons, matching narrow hip-level belt, large grey-pink textured Crimplene-jersey collar, flared mini-skirt in matching fabric. Grey suede sling-back shoes, high vamps, square toes, flat heels.

Evening Wear

1 Cream Terylene-crepe evening dress, unfitted bodice and full-length flared skirt gathered from under outsized pearl bead trim around high round neckline, no waist seam, cut-away armholes. Cream pearlized-leather shoes, large buckle trim, almond-shaped toes. 2 Yellow silk-crepe mini-length unfitted shift dress, cut-away armholes, high round neckline trimmed with loops of fine yellow silk-velvet ribbon to match two rows around hemline of flared skirt. Yellow satin sling-back shoes, almond-shaped toes, low thick heels. 3 Black mohair and silk evening suit: high three-button single-breasted fastening under narrow satin-faced shawl collar, matching covered buttons, piped pockets; tapered trousers, braid trim on outer side seams, no turn-ups. White silk collar-attached shirt. Narrow black satin bow-tie. Black leather lace-up shoes, almond-shaped toes. 4 Mint-green silk-chiffon evening dress, unfitted bodice and full-length skirt gathered from under cut-away armholes and high round neckline, no waist seam, neckline and armholes decorated with tiny green and silver silk flowers, matching band above hemline of skirt; underdress of mint-green silk follows same lines as chiffon dress. Silver kid shoes, almond-shaped toes. 5 Lilac silk shift dress, unfitted bodice and mini-skirt decorated with bands of royal-blue sequins, full-length inset sleeves embroidered all over with matching sequins, hems bound in lilac satin to match wide square neckline and narrow hemline of skirt. Royal-blue suede shoes, gold kid sling-backs and T-straps, almond-shaped toes, low thick heels.

Sports and Leisure Wear

1 Beach wear. Green, white and red striped cotton draped bra top, low neckline, knot of self-fabric between seamed cups, draped cut-away front, bare midriff, narrow shoulder strap. Long bias-cut striped sash in matching fabric tied on side hip over green cotton hipster trousers, tight over hips and upper legs, flared from knee-level to hemline. 2 Sailing. Fitted white knitted-cotton shirt, pointed collar, keyhole opening, loop-and-button fastening, short inset sleeves, top-stitched hems. Navy-blue cotton sailcloth hipster shorts, fly-front, piped side hip pockets, high-cut legs, wide red leather belt, large metal buckle. White cotton peaked cap, navy-blue ribbon trim. 3 Golf. Beige, brown and orange checked wool two-piece: single-breasted shirt top, pointed collar worn turned up, full-length inset sleeves, buttoned cuffs; flared mini-skirt, centre-front inverted box-pleat, wide waistband, self-fabric belt, metal buckle. Beige knee-high wool socks. Brown leather bar-strap shoes, round toes. 4 Holiday wear. White Crimplene-jersey sleeveless dress, wide round neckline bound in black to match hemline of straight mini-length skirt, pointed edges of cropped hipster skirt and bow trim where points meet on centre-front, bare midriff. Black leather sling-back shoes, almond-shaped toes, low thick heels. 5 Casual wear. Multicoloured spotted Bri-nylon stretch top, high round neckline, full-length inset sleeves, matching tights, wide headband and narrow tie-belt on white plastic 'leather-look' hipster mini-skirt. Long white plastic boots, square toes, flat heels.

Underwear and Negligee

1 Green, blue and grey striped silk dressing gown, wrapover front, self-fabric tie-belt, full-length inset sleeves, turned-back cuffs, large hip-level patch pockets, breast pocket. Blue cotton-poplin pyjamas: single-breasted jacket; ankle-length straight-cut trousers. Navy-blue leather slippers, round toes. 2 Red cotton mini-length nightdress, black satin peter-pan collar, black lace edging to match waterfall jabot, two-tier circular-cut cuffs of elbow-length inset sleeves and hemline trim. 3 Pink cotton mini-length nightdress, pale-blue and white pattern of flowers, skirt and bodice gathered from under wide neckline bound with pink satin ribbon, bow trim, lace edging matching centre-front mock strap-and-button fastening, lace trimmed hemline, cut-away armholes. 4 Pale-blue Crimplene negligee and nightdress: negligee with lace-effect from under bust, elbow-length kimono-style sleeves, all hems and edges bound with blue satin ribbon matching bow trim on centre-front under bust, full-length skirts gathered from high waist position; nightdress with lace-effect fitted bodice, low neckline, high waistline, full-length flared skirt. 5 Black Lycra and lace body suit, narrow shoulder straps, low neckline, half cups, wide lace trim, panelled body, high-cut legs, lace trim, four suspenders. Flesh-coloured nylon stockings. 6 Black Lycra body suit, multicoloured spot pattern, fine shoulder straps, keyhole between seamed cups, long legs.

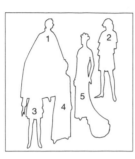
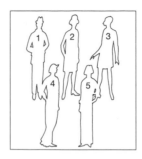
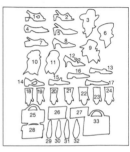

1967 Day Wear

1 Navy-blue wool two-piece suit: hip-length unfitted jacket, double-breasted fastening under wide round neckline, brass buttons, matching epaulets and flap pockets, three-quarter-length inset sleeves, top-stitched edges and detail; flared mini-skirt. Navy-blue wool polo-neck infill. Yellow wool peaked cap. Short navy-blue leather gloves; matching knee-high boots, round toes, flat heels. 2 White cotton two-piece trouser suit with multicoloured pattern of flowers and leaves: long fitted jacket, double-breasted fastening, stand-away collar, pointed lapels, welt pockets; flared trousers, turn-ups. Lilac cotton polo-neck sweater. Purple leather bar-strap shoes, round toes, flat heels. 3 Mid-grey wool and Terylene unfitted jacket flecked with black, high four-button single-breasted fastening, narrow lapels, three patch pockets, leather-covered buttons, top-stitched edges and detail. Dark-grey wool and Terylene tapered trousers, permanent creases, no turn-ups. Black wool polo-neck sweater. Black leather elastic-sided ankle-boots. 4 Grey flannel dress, unfitted hip-length bodice, detachable white cotton collar matching cuffs of three-quarter-length inset sleeves, black silk scarf-tie, hip-level wide black leather belt, large metal buckle, straight mini-skirt. Black leather T-strap shoes, almond-shaped toes. 5 Bright-yellow cotton-canvas semi-fitted coat, flared skirt, pointed lapels, long collar, single-breasted fastening with triangular yellow plastic buttons matching trim on triangular flap pockets, long inset sleeves, top-stitched edges and detail. Yellow plastic beret. Knee-high white cotton socks. Navy-blue leather-look plastic shoulder bag, short gloves and step-in shoes.

Wedding Wear

1 White silk wedding dress, semi-fitted bodice and ankle-length straight skirt cut without waist seam, cut-away armholes, ground-length white silk-organdie cape gathered from high round neckline under frilled organdie stand collar, cape scattered with silk flowers matching silk and organdie bonnet. White kid shoes, square toes. 2 White cotton broderie-anglaise wedding dress, straight neckline with scalloped and embroidered edge above high yoke seam matching three-tier gathered three-quarter-length inset sleeves and hemline of flared mini-skirt. White velvet choker. White suede T-strap shoes, almond-shaped toes, low thick heels. 3 White pintucked cotton wedding dress, bloused bodice, pintucked cotton-organza and lace yoke edged with frilled lace continuing over bishop-style sleeves in matching fabric, deep cuffs with frilled hems matching high stand collar, gathered mini-skirt, band of pintucked organza and lace above hemline, white satin belt, bow tie on side waist. Hair decorated with white organza flowers. White satin shoes, bow trim, almond-shaped toes. 4 Pale-turquoise velvet wedding dress, high neckline split on centre-front seam, full-length inset sleeves, high waist position marked by wide pale-turquoise silk belt, bow tie on centre-front, ground-length flared skirt. Pearl tiara; long silk-tulle veil. Pale-turquoise satin shoes. 5 Fine cream wool-crepe wedding dress, high round neckline, short inset sleeves, semi-fitted bodice, no waist seam, ground-length skirt, long back train. Long cream silk-tulle veil attached to headdress of peach-pink roses. Short cream kid gloves; matching shoes.

Sports and Leisure Wear

1 Country wear. Short weatherproof green cotton overcoat, front-zip fastening from above hemline to ends of wide collar, full-length inset sleeves, vertical welt pockets above hip-level patch pockets, buttoned flaps, top-stitched edges and detail. Tapered dark-green wool trousers, narrow hems, no turn-ups. Brown wool polo-neck sweater. Green and brown checked trilby, small crown, self-fabric band, narrow brim. Brown waterproofed suede lace-up ankle-boots. 2 Holiday wear. Sleeveless cotton dress, hip-length plain white unfitted bodice, high round neckline, dark-blue and red striped mini-skirt, low side-hip pockets, slotted self-fabric belt, button trim. Red and white striped hat, high crown, wide turned-up brim. Red leather sling-back shoes, round toes, strap detail, low thick heels. 3 Holiday wear. Mini-length sleeveless rayon shift dress with multicoloured Pop-Art design, high round neckline, bound hemline and cut-away armholes. Purple leather sling-back shoes, round toes, low thick heels. 4 Golf. Brown waist-length knitted-wool collarless cardigan, edges and hem in dark-beige matching welt pockets and deep welts of full-length inset sleeves, large plastic buttons. Burnt-orange wool trousers fitted over hips, flared from knee to hem, side hip pockets. Cream wool shirt, long pointed collar. Orange leather-look plastic peaked cap. Tan and white leather lace-up brogues, flat heels. 5 Holiday wear. Two-piece cotton beach pyjamas patterned in lime-greens, royal-blues and bright-pinks: hip-length unfitted bias-cut top, high round neckline, three-quarter-length inset sleeves, deep turned-back cuffs; wide straight-cut trousers. Green canvas sling-back shoes, round toes, flat heels.

Accessories

1 Cream leather sling-back strap sandals, low heels. 2 Red leather sling-back strap sandals, medium heels. 3 Beige felt hat, high crown, wide brim. 4 Grey shoes, twisted strap fronts, flat heels. 5 Navy-blue sling-back shoes, high heels. 6 White straw hat, wide brim, red ribbon binding. 7 Brown leather sling-back sandals, cross-strap fronts, perforated decoration, wedge heels. 8 Green leather shoes, draped side detail, high heels. 9 White canvas peaked cap, navy-blue and red ribbon trim, brass button detail. 10 Blue and white striped cotton peaked cap. 11 Red wool beret. 12 Red leather shoes, black leather bar strap, ribbon bow trim, high heels. 13 Black patent-leather shoes, velvet bow trim, flat heels. 14 Black leather shoes, cream T-strap and trim. 15 White leather bar-strap shoes, blue trim. 16 White leather shoes, red Pop-Art patterned toe-caps. 17 Brown leather shoes, cream uppers. 18 Cream leather gloves, navy-blue trim. 19 Red and black leather gloves. 20 Beige fabric gloves, black spots. 21 Red leather gloves, navy-blue and white detail. 22 Dark-green leather gloves, purple trim. 23 White cotton gloves, black and white checked cuffs. 24 Grey plastic gloves, black trim. 25 Green and grey checked canvas handbag, flap, clasp fastening, leather handles. 26 Black leather bag, suede trim. 27 Black and white leather envelope-shaped bag. 28 Blue plastic handbag, two outside pockets, buttoned flaps, flap, concealed fastening, flat handle. 29 White leather shoes, square toes, black Pop-Art trim. 30 Green leather shoes, brass-buckle trim. 31 Black leather shoes, square toes, black and white checked buckle trim. 32 Cream leather shoes, brown toe-caps and trim. 33 Tan leather handbag, two outside pockets, flap, clasp fastening, flat handles.

1968 Day Wear

1 Navy-blue wool and Terylene two-piece suit: fitted double-breasted jacket, flap pockets, no breast pocket, sewn cuffs; top-stitched edges and detail; tapered trousers, narrow hems, permanent creases, no turn-ups. Pale-blue cotton collar-attached shirt. Wide silk tie, blue and red stripes, Windsor knot. Black leather shoes, strap-and-buckle fastening. **2** Beige and brown flecked silk-tweed sleeveless dress, high round neckline, wide brown leather waist-level belt slotted through two mock box-pleats running from bust-level yoke seam to hemline of flared mini-length skirt, top-stitched edges and detail. Brown leather sling-back shoes, round toes, bar straps, low thick heels. **3** Pale-grey wool mini-length coat patterned in pale-blues, pinks and greens, strap-and-buckle fastening from waist-level to under stand collar, full-length two-piece inset sleeves, large hip-level patch-and-flap pockets, top-stitched edges and detail. Short pale-grey leather gloves; matching over-knee-length boots, strap-and-buckle trim, inside-leg zip fastening, round toes, low square heels. **4** Red wool maxi-length coat, fitted double-breasted bodice fastening under large collar, full-length inset sleeves, edge-to-edge flared skirts, hip-level welt pockets. Brimless black fur hat. Black plastic 'leather-look' over-the-knee boots, mock-lacing on centre-front seam, round toes, low heels. **5** Pink synthetic-silk-crepe dress, hip-length semi-fitted bodice, horizontal tucks, strap-and-button fastening under pointed collar, full-length sleeves gathered into deep cuffs, knife-pleated mini-skirt. Pale-pink nylon tights. Grey and white leather shoes, round toes.

Evening Wear

1 Winter dinner/theatre ensemble: fine white cotton blouse, semi-fitted bodice, ruffled frill either side mock-buttoned strap fastening, self-fabric covered buttons, pintucked stand collar with frilled edge matching cuffs of full-length bishop-style sleeves; ankle-length yellow, red and black checked wool skirt, black leather belt, metal clasp fastening. Black leather shoes, round toes, buckle trim, low thick heels. **2** Gold and bronze synthetic fabric evening dress, floor-length accordion-pleated skirt and fitted bodice, high waist position marked by narrow gold kid belt, wide neckline with trim of gold, bronze and crystal beads which continues over shoulders to hems of full-length inset sleeves. **3** Navy-blue wool and mohair two-piece evening suit: fitted jacket, edge-to-edge linked-button fastening, long shawl collar faced in silk and edged with braid, piped pockets, no breast pocket, two side vents; tapered trousers, narrow hems, no turn-ups, braid trim on outside seams. White cotton collar-attached shirt. Navy-blue silk bow-tie. Navy-blue suede ankle-boots. **4** Pale-grey silk-crepe two-piece evening suit with self-colour satin pattern: unfitted mini-length tunic, full-length inset sleeves gathered into deep cuffs, hip-level welt pockets, chain belt set with black stones, detachable self-fabric scarf; narrow ankle-length trousers. Black velvet mules, almond-shaped toes, eyelet trim, low thick heels. **5** Canary-yellow fine wool-crepe cocktail dress, semi-fitted bodice and flared mini-length skirt cut without waist seam, high round neckline edged with beads matching cut-away V-shaped armholes and hemline. Gold kid shoes, almond-shaped toes, low thick heels.

Sports and Leisure Wear

1 Casual wear. Tan wool fine-knit polo-neck sweater, fitted body, machined welt, low-slung belt, half-ring and chain fastening, full-length inset sleeves, buttoned cuffs. Fitted brown cotton trousers flared from knee-level to hem, no turn-ups. Dark-yellow leather cowboy boots, pointed toes, stacked heels. **2** Tennis. White knitted-cotton T-shirt, high round neckline, short inset sleeves. White cotton-poplin shorts, side hip pockets, deep waistband, self-fabric belt, metal clasp fastening. White cotton peaked cap, wide visor. White ankle socks. White canvas sports shoes. **3** Holiday wear. Pale-blue towelling two-piece beach suit: edge-to-edge collarless jacket banded in blue and white, three-quarter-length inset sleeves, single breast patch pocket, self-fabric tie-belt; fitted shorts, elasticated waistband, mock fly-front. **4** Country wear. Dark-rust-brown edge-to-edge sheepskin coat, cream lambswool collar and lining matching turned-back cuffs of full-length inset sleeves, mini-length flared skirts. Beige knitted-wool polo-neck sweater. Camel-coloured wool fitted shorts, top-stitched creases, brown leather belt. Rust-brown wool tights. Brown leather knee-high boots, round toes, flat heels. **5** Beach wear. Red plastic bikini: small asymmetric bra top, single shoulder strap and armhole bound in silver plastic to match appliqué spot on one side, edges and zipped side pocket of fitted shorts. **6** Beach wear. Blue and white striped cotton unfitted top, boat-shaped neckline, wide three-quarter-length two-piece sleeves, buttoned outside seams, deep white plastic belt matches buttons. Red cotton headscarf.

Underwear and Negligee

1 Salmon-pink nylon combination bra and semi-fitted slip, underwired bra cups, wide adjustable shoulder straps, low neckline edges with self-colour nylon lace matching trim on edge of side front panel seams running from under bust to flared hemline of mini-length skirt. **2** White cotton mini-length collarless edge-to-edge negligee, self-colour satin spot pattern, ribbon fastening on centre-front at bust-level matching ribbon trim on front edges, detail above double broderie-anglaise frill on elbow-length inset sleeves, under neckline of matching nightdress and above two-tier frills of broderie-anglaise trimming on hemlines of nightdress and negligee. **3** Two-piece pale-green knitted-cotton sleepsuit: hip-length top, V-shaped neckline bound in dark-green matching cuffs of full-length inset sleeves, hemline of top and cuffs of ankle-length trousers. **4** White knitted-cotton T-shirt, high round neckline, short inset sleeves. Y-front briefs in matching fabric, elasticated waistband, high-cut legs. **5** Flesh-coloured stretch-nylon all-in-one body stocking, low neckline, narrow shoulder straps, high-cut legs. **6** Synthetic-silk dressing gown, multicoloured pattern on black background, long shawl collar, wrapover front, self-fabric tie-belt, full-length inset sleeves, turned-back cuffs, two large hip-level patch pockets, knee-length skirts. Ankle-length black pyjama trousers. Black leather step-in slippers.

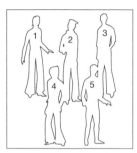

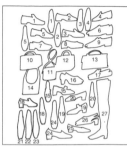

1969 Day Wear

1 Pink Crimplene collarless coatdress, high round neckline, high waist position marked by narrow self-fabric belt, round buckle, concealed fastening under scalloped wrapover front, matching hemline, fitted full-length inset sleeves. Pale-grey felt hat, high crown, black band, wide brim. Black leather gloves and sling-back shoes, square toes, low thick heels. **2** Red wool maxi-length coat, fitted bodice and flared skirts cut without waist seam, top-stitched double-breasted front panel under black fake-fur collar, collar matches cuffs of full-length inset sleeves and brimless hat, hip-length shaped flap pockets, button trim. Ankle-length straight-cut black wool trousers. Black leather boots, round toes, low thick heels. **3** Dark-green wool double-breasted overcoat, large black fur collar matching sleeve cuffs, hip-level shaped flap pockets. Black Terylene and wool flared trousers, no turn-ups. Green flannel collar-attached shirt worn open. Grey, green, orange and black patterned silk scarf. Black leather ankle-boots. **4** Cream, blue-grey and charcoal-grey checked wool-jersey two-piece suit: edge-to-edge waist-length box-shaped jacket, long collar, full-length inset sleeves gathered into cuffs, mock-flap pockets, button trim matching pockets on hipline of flared mini-skirt, centre-front knife-pleat. Cream synthetic-silk blouse, scarf-tie neckline. Knee-high cream cotton stockings. Black leather step-in shoes, square toes, flat heels. **5** Rust-red and grey checked wool semi-fitted dress, vertical inset stripe on centre-front of plain cream wool running from under narrow shaped stand collar to horizontal stripe on hipline, matching stripes above bust and waistline and as cuffs on full-length inset sleeves. Brown leather strap sandals, low thick heels.

Evening Wear

1 Pale-yellow silk-crepe two-piece evening dress, hip-length semi-fitted top, high round neckline embroidered with gold and white beads to match detail either side centre-front seam, edges and hem of skirt, armhole seams, wrist trim of long inset sleeves, low waist tie-belt and hems of ankle-length straight-cut trousers. Yellow satin shoes, square toes, high tongues, gold embroidery trim, low thick heels. **2** Navy-blue velvet fitted jacket, green and red stripe pattern of leaves and flowers, two-button single-breasted fastening, flap pockets. Navy-blue wool and mohair flared trousers, no turn-ups. White collar-attached shirt, ruffled front; navy-blue velvet bow-tie worn under wide-set shirt collar. Black leather lace-up shoes. **3** Fine black wool-crepe ankle-length evening dress, semi-fitted bodice and straight skirt cut without waist seam, skirt split on one side to above knee-level, tight full-length inset sleeves, high round neckline. Short sleeveless bolero jacket, low scooped neckline, black, red and gold bead embroidery. Black satin shoes, almond-shaped toes, high heels. **4** Jade-green satin evening dress, semi-fitted bodice and full-length flared skirt cut without waist seam, high polo collar, halter-style cut-away armholes. Black and jade-green feather boa. Jade-green satin pumps, round toes. **5** Black silk two-piece evening suit: knee-length single-breasted fitted jacket worn open, four-button fastening under high lapels, hip-level welt pockets in flared skirts; narrow ankle-length trousers in matching fabric. Collarless single-breasted gold and black brocade waistcoat. White silk polo-neck shirt. Black satin ankle-boots, round toes, low thick heels.

Sports and Leisure Wear

1 Golf. Grey, forest-green and brown checked wool sleeveless jumpsuit, semi-fitted bodice, single-breasted fastening under V-shaped neckline, bell-bottom trousers, narrow hip-level green leather belt, matching covered buttons. Grey knitted-wool sweater, ribbed polo collar, body and full-length inset sleeves. Brown leather step-in shoes, round toes, flat heels. **2** Golf. Pale-fawn mock-suede waist-length jacket, zip fastening to under brown knitted-wool collar which matches side panels of fitted waistband, full-length inset sleeves, buttoned cuffs, vertical welt pockets under yoke seam. Light-brown wool trousers fitted over hips, flared from knee-level, side hip pockets. Tan knitted-wool polo-neck sweater. Fawn wool-tweed peaked cap. Dark-brown leather ankle-boots. **3** Leisure wear. Unfitted black cotton top, round neckline and loop-and-button fastening edged with rows of gold and black braid matching trim on shoulder seams, elbow-length inset sleeves and hemline, wide black leather belt, large brass buckle. Black cotton bell-bottom trousers, no turn-ups. **4** Country wear. Camel-coloured wool hip-length jacket, sheepskin lining, zip fastening from hemline to under neck of hood, full-length inset sleeves, self-fabric belt, large hip-level patch-and-flap pockets. Brown wool bell-bottom trousers. Brown leather round-toed boots, flat heels. **5** Casual wear. Blue and white spotted cotton-voile shirt, pointed collar worn open. Fitted blue brushed-cotton trousers, curved side-hip pockets, black leather belt, large metal buckle. Red silk neckscarf and multicoloured bead necklace. Knee-high brown leather boots.

Accessories

1 Beige leather step-in shoes, high tongues. **2** Tan leather step-in shoes, high tongues, strap-and-stud trim. **3** Grey leather step-in shoes, high tongues, strap-and-ring trim. **4** Navy-blue leather step-in shoes, strap with tassel-tie trim, square toes. **5** Black velvet step-in evening shoes. **6** Dark-green leather lace-up shoes, ruched detail. **7** Black leather step-in shoes, strap-and-buckle fastening. **8** Black leather lace-up shoes, stitched fronts. **9** Black and white leather lace-up shoes. **10** Olive-green leather bag, black and red inset stripe, brass clasp and trim. **11** Red plastic shoulder bag, zipped top pocket over buckled strap and flap. **12** Cream plastic leather-look bag, top zip fastening, front flap pocket, double self-fabric handles. **13** Beige canvas bag, flap edged in green webbing to match straps and trim, brass fittings, single handle. **14** Yellow plastic bag, long handle, top zip pocket matching front pocket. **15** Navy-blue and cream leather T-strap shoes, perforated decoration. **16** Black leather shoes, high thick heels, round toes, thin platform soles. **17** Brown mock-suede mules, peep toes, cut-out detail, low wedge heels, thin platform soles. **18** Navy-blue leather shoes, high tongues, large square buckle trim, low stacked heels. **19** Brown and black leather bar-strap shoes, low stacked heels. **20** Cream plastic leather-look shoes, button trim, stacked heels. **21** Grey leather shoes, strap-and-button trim. **22** Red leather shoes, trimmed linked rings. **23** Black patent-leather shoes, large round buckle trim. **24** Tan leather shoes, fringed tongues, low heels. **25** Pale-grey leather lace-up shoes, low heels. **26** Navy-blue and red leather sling-back shoes, perforated decoration, low heels. **27** Thigh-length black plastic boots, stretch uppers, patent-look shoes.

Chart of the Development of 1960s Fashion

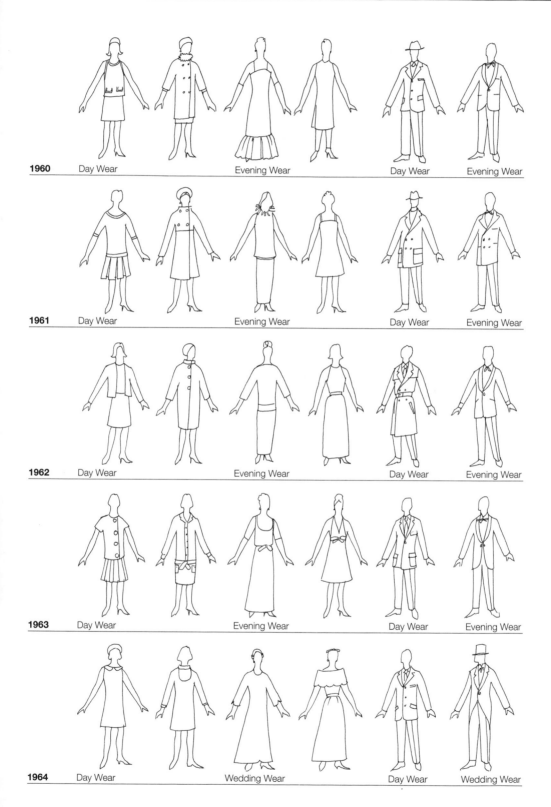

| 1960 | Day Wear | | Evening Wear | | Day Wear | Evening Wear |

| 1961 | Day Wear | | Evening Wear | | Day Wear | Evening Wear |

| 1962 | Day Wear | | Evening Wear | | Day Wear | Evening Wear |

| 1963 | Day Wear | | Evening Wear | | Day Wear | Evening Wear |

| 1964 | Day Wear | | Wedding Wear | | Day Wear | Wedding Wear |

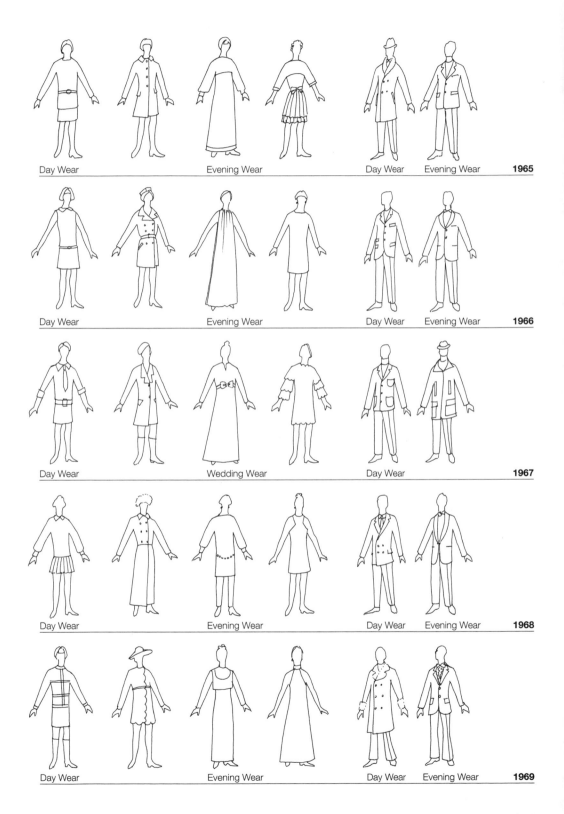

| Day Wear | Evening Wear | Day Wear | Evening Wear | **1965** |

| Day Wear | Evening Wear | Day Wear | Evening Wear | **1966** |

| Day Wear | Wedding Wear | Day Wear | | **1967** |

| Day Wear | Evening Wear | Day Wear | Evening Wear | **1968** |

| Day Wear | Evening Wear | Day Wear | Evening Wear | **1969** |

Biographies of Designers

Balenciaga, Cristobal
1895–1972. Designer. Born
Guetaria, Spain. At the age of
twenty Balenciaga opened his
first house in San Sebastian.
When he moved to Paris in 1936
he was already Spain's leading
couturier, producing austere,
elegant, well-cut clothes in
sombre colours recognizable for
their stark Spanish style. In 1939
his tight-waisted dresses with
dropped shoulderlines were clear
forerunners of Dior's New Look.
His many innovations include the
pillbox hat, the stand-away collar,
and the sack dress of 1956.
In the 1960s he was one of
the first couturiers to design
bodystockings and produced
highly successful loose jackets
with dolman sleeves. His couture
house closed in 1968.

Bates, John 1938–. Designer.
Born Ponteland, England. Bates
started the company Jean Varon
in the early 1960s and soon
became known as one of that
decade's most audacious
designers, producing the briefest
of mini-skirts, trouser suits,
catsuits and broderie-anglaise
eveningwear. He also made
garments from Op Art-inspired
fabrics. Among his most widely
copied designs were a black
leather outfit and a white vinyl
coat he created for the actress
Diana Rigg in the British TV series
The Avengers.

Beene, Geoffrey 1927–.
Designer. Born Haynesville,
Louisiana, USA. Beene studied at
the Traphagen School of Fashion,
New York. In the late 1940s he
moved to Paris where he trained
at the Académie Julian and at
Molyneux. On his return to New
York in 1948, he worked for
a number of ready-to-wear
companies before he founded
his own firm in 1963. Beene
designs graphically striking
garments which combine couture
quality with the ease of modern
sportswear. He has shown
originality in mixing fabrics and in
the use of synthetic materials.

Blass, Bill 1922–. Designer.
Born Fort Wayne, Indiana, USA.
After World War II Blass joined
Anne Miller & Co. who merged
with Maurice Rentner Ltd in
1959. He became vice president
in 1962 and from 1970 the
company went under his own
name. During the 1960s Blass
was known for his dresses
extravagantly trimmed with ruffles
and lace. Though he often

borrows from the male wardrobe
for his sportswear, Blass tailors
his suits with a curved silhouette
which flatters the female shape.

Bohan, Marc 1926–. Designer.
Born Paris, France. Bohan
worked freelance for Piguet,
Molyneux and Patou, among
others, before he was appointed
director of Dior's English
operations in London in 1958.
In 1961 he succeeded Saint
Laurent as head designer in
Paris. He quickly established a
reputation for maintaining the
refined, romantic image of Dior
while adapting popular, youthful
styles to haute couture. Among
his most influential designs of the
1960s were the cossack-style
fur-trimmed coats and full skirts
he created in 1966. He is best
known for his elegant evening
gowns in rich fabrics.

Cardin, Pierre 1922–. Designer.
Born San Biago de Callalta, near
Venice, Italy. Cardin worked for
a tailor in Vichy from the age of
seventeen. He moved to Paris
in 1944 and found work with
Paquin, Dior and Schiaparelli.
He opened his own house in
1950. By the 1960s he had
developed into a highly innovative
and influential designer for men
and women. His designs were
bold and uncompromising:
cut-out dresses, mini-skirts,
brightly coloured wigs and
dresses with necklines cut to
the navel. In 1964 he showed
his 'Space Age' collection which
included catsuits, batwing
jumpsuits and helmets.

Cashin, Bonnie 1915–.
Designer. Born Oakland,
California, USA. Cashin began
her career as a costume designer
before opening her own business
in New York in 1953. She created
casual, practical clothes. During
the 1960s she introduced the
idea of layered dressing and
was acclaimed for mixing natural
fabrics such as leather, linen and
cashmere. She was also known
for her Chinese-style jackets,
fringed suede dresses and
stylish ponchos.

Cassini, Oleg 1913–. Designer.
Born Paris, France, of Russian
parents. Cassini worked in Paris,
New York and Hollywood before
opening his own firm in 1950. He
became famous for glamorous
ready-to-wear suits and sheath
and cocktail dresses. He was
appointed official designer to
Jacqueline Kennedy (Onassis) in

1961. The two-piece suit with
three-quarter length sleeves he
made for her was widely copied.

Castillo, Antonio 1908–.
Designer. Born Madrid, Spain.
Castillo designed dresses, hats
and jewelry for Paquin and Piguet
from 1936 until 1945 when he
joined Elizabeth Arden's salon
in New York. Returning to Paris
in 1950, he was made designer
for the house of Lanvin. Castillo
founded his own company
in 1964. He was known for
luxurious, elegant garments
with intricate detail.

Clark, Ossie 1942–96. Designer.
Born Liverpool, England. From
1957 to 1961 Clark attended
Manchester College of Art and
the Royal College of Art in
London. He began designing
for the boutique Quorum while
still a student and became a full-
time designer in 1966. Clark was
responsible for some of the most
innovative styles of the 1960s,
including hot-pants, maxi coats
and gypsy-style dresses.

Courrèges, André 1923–.
Designer. Born Pau, France. After
studying engineering, Courrèges
joined Balenciaga in 1945. In
1961 he set up his own house.
Courrèges fused the precise
technique he had learnt at
Balenciaga with the functionalism
of his training as an engineer to
produce some of the most avant-
garde designs of the 1960s. His
early collections included mini
dresses and trouser suits in white
and silver, futuristic accessories
such as goggles, and his famous
white mid-calf boots. In the late
1960s he produced catsuits and
cut-out dresses.

de la Renta, Oscar 1932–.
Designer. Born Santo Domingo,
Dominican Republic. De la Renta
studied at the Academia de San
Fernando in Madrid. His first
design, a debutante gown for the
daughter of the US ambassador
to Spain, was featured on the
cover of *Life* and led to a job
with Balenciaga. After a period
at Lanvin and Jane Derby, he
founded his own house in 1965.
De la Renta is best known for
his dramatic evening wear,
often lavishly trimmed. His
1967 Gypsy collection was a
precursor to the 1970s vogue
for peasant styles.

Fratini, Gina 1934–. Designer.
Born Kobe, Japan, of English
parents. Fratini studied fashion
at the Royal College of Art in

London. From her first collection
in 1966, she became known for
an essentially romantic style,
expressed in frilly, floating dresses
and flowing evening gowns.

Galanos, James 1924–.
Designer. Born Philadelphia,
USA. Galanos was apprenticed
to Piguet in Paris in 1947, and in
1951 founded his own company
in Los Angeles. His first show
in 1953 brought immediate
success. He is known for his high
standards of tailoring and for his
use of luxurious fabrics. During
the 1960s he designed many
close-fitting, classically draped
evening dresses.

Galitzine, Princess Irene
1916–. Designer. Born Tiflis,
Russia. Galitzine studied art and
design in Rome. From the mid-
1940s she worked for Fontana
until she set up her own business
in 1949. In 1960 she introduced
her most famous design, the
wide-legged 'Palazzo Pyjamas'.
Galitzine produced garments that
epitomized 1960s Italian high
style: open-sided dresses, toga
tops worn over trousers and, in
1966, a futuristic quilted vinyl
jumpsuit. In 1968 she turned to
freelance designing but reopened
her house under the name
'Princess Galitzine' in 1970.

Gernreich, Rudi 1922–85.
Designer. Born Vienna, Austria.
Gernreich began designing for
the Los Angeles boutique Jax
in 1948 and started his own
firm in 1964. He is considered
the most radical of the 1960s
American designers. Among
his most experimental designs
were jackets with one notched
and one rounded lapel and
elasticated swimsuits with
no inner structuring. In 1964
he launched the 'no-bra bra'
which allowed a natural body
shape, the highly controversial
topless bathing suit and a
flesh-coloured bodystocking in
stretch nylon. He also promoted
unisex clothing with designs for
kaftans, bell-bottom trousers
and cropped tops.

Givenchy, Hubert de 1927–.
Designer. Born Beauvais, France.
Givenchy worked for Fath,
Piguet, Lelong and Schiaparelli
before opening his own business
in 1952. During the 1950s his
young, playful style became more
sombre under the influence of
Balenciaga. Givenchy was hugely
influential, particularly through his
designs for Audrey Hepburn in

the 1961 film *Breakfast at Tiffany's*. During the 1960s his chic, simple and highly wearable designs became increasingly sophisticated.

Halston, Roy 1932–. Designer. Born Des Moines, Iowa, USA. Halston opened a millinery salon in 1953 in Chicago before moving to New York in 1958 to work for Lily Daché and then for Bergdorf Goodman. He founded a ready-to-wear firm in 1966, gaining a reputation for sexy, glamorous clothes with a slim silhouette. He was influential in the late 1960s with sophisticated designs for halterneck jumpsuits and dresses, wide-legged trousers and cashmere sweaters.

Hulanicki, Barbara 1936–. Designer. Born Palestine, of Polish parents. After studying at Brighton Art College, Hulanicki won a London *Evening Standard* competition for beachwear in 1955. She then worked as an illustrator for various magazines, including *Vogue* and *Tatler*. Hulanicki sold her first designs by mail order. In 1964 she opened her Biba shop in Kensington which became famous for its stylishly decadent atmosphere with lavish decor inspired by 1930s interiors and art nouveau. Here, affordable mini skirts and unisex T-shirts dyed in rich, muted colours were eagerly snapped up by a young clientele. Other signature items include floppy felt hats, feather boas and velvet trouser suits.

Johnson, Betsey 1942–. Designer. Born Hartford, Connecticut, USA. Johnson studied fine art at Syracuse University in New York and was appointed guest editor of *Mademoiselle* in 1964. She then worked as a freelance designer and in 1965 began supplying the New York shop Paraphernalia. During the 1960s she produced inexpensive, inventive garments such as a transparent vinyl dress with adhesive star motifs, a silver motorcycle suit and a 'noise' dress fringed with grommets. Her cowhide mini skirts and slinky T-shirt dresses were also popular. In 1969 she opened a boutique called Betsey, Bunkey, and Nini.

Khanh, Emanuelle 1937–. Designer. Born Paris, France. Khanh began her career in fashion in the 1950s as a model for Balenciaga and Givenchy.

Her success as a designer was assured when an article featuring her 'Yé Yé' styles in a 1961 edition of *Elle*. During the 1960s she created collections for various houses, including Dorothée Bis, Cacharel, Missoni and Krizia. Khanh was at the forefront of young Parisian fashion, producing feminine designs with a nostalgic 1930s feel. She was known for close-fitting jackets and dresses, sometimes featuring long collars.

Missoni, Ottavio and Rosita Knitwear designers. Ottavio born 1921 in Dalmatia; Rosita born 1931 in Lombardy, Italy. After founding the Missoni company in 1953, the couple produced their first knitwear collection for Rinascente Stores in 1954. In 1958 they launched their own label. They rose to prominence in the 1960s and 1970s, creating fluid, boldly patterned dresses, coats and sweaters which restored the fashion world's interest in knitwear. Missoni is known for sophisticated knitting techniques and an artistic blending of colour.

Muir, Jean 1933–95. Designer. Born London, England. After working at Liberty, where she eventually became a sketcher, Muir joined Jaeger in 1956. In 1962 she began designing a line called Jane & Jane. She set up her own company in 1966. Muir used an exceptionally fine technique to create fluid, timeless clothes in jersey and suede.

Norell, Norman 1900–72. Designer. Born Noblesville, USA. From 1922 Norell worked as a costume designer and for the Seventh Avenue firm Charles Armour. In 1928 he joined Hattie Carnegie, where he remained until he founded Traina-Norell with Anthony Traina in 1941. During the 1940s and 1950s Norell made his reputation as one of America's finest designers. He was best known for stylish, elaborate eveningwear, especially his sequined sheath dresses. Norell opened his own house in 1960, launching his famous culotte suit in the same year.

Pucci, Emilio 1914–85. Designer. Born Naples, Italy. In the mid-1940s, as a member of the Italian Olympic ski team, Pucci was photographed by Toni Frissell for *Harper's Bazaar* wearing ski pants he had designed himself. The magazine

then published some of his designs for women's winter clothes which were quickly bought by several New York stores. He founded his own couture house, Emilio, in 1950, producing capri pants and other casual wear. Pucci created prints inspired by medieval heraldic banners – psychedelic designs which are now synonymous with the fashions of the 1960s.

Quant, Mary 1934–. Designer. Born London, England. Quant attended Goldsmith's College of Art in London. In 1955 she worked briefly for the milliner Erik and later that year opened a boutique in Chelsea called Bazaar. Quant was perfectly in tune with the needs of her young, hip clientele. Her inexpensive, classless designs revolutionized dress for the teenage market and created an entirely British look. Items such as mini skirts, short pinafore dresses and skinny-rib polo-neck sweaters were all popularized by Quant. She also promoted PVC garments and crocheted tops. From 1963 Quant's designs were mass-produced for the US market, where her style was hugely influential.

Rabanne, Paco 1934–. Designer. Born San Sebastian, Spain. After studying architecture at the Ecole des Beaux-Arts in Paris, Rabanne sold designs for plastic jewelry and buttons to Balenciaga, Dior and Givenchy. In 1964 he caused a sensation with the launch of a futuristic plastic dress, the first of many designs to introduce alternative materials. Rabanne opened his own house in 1966, creating garments made of paper, aluminium and chainmail in a process akin to industrial design. He was also inventive in his mixing of leather, fur and knitted wool.

Rhodes, Zandra 1940–. Designer. Born Chatham, Kent, England. In 1961 Rhodes attended the Royal College of Art in London. She first sold her designs from her shop in London. In 1968 she founded her own house and in 1969 *Vogue* featured her designs for chiffon scarves, caftans and dresses with handkerchief points. Taking her handprinted fabrics as the starting point for her clothes, Rhodes became famous for fantastic, floating garments in silk and chiffon.

Saint Laurent, Yves 1936–. Designer. Born Oran, Algeria. Saint Laurent won first prize for a design for a cocktail dress in a competition held by the International Wool Secretariat in 1954. In 1955 he began working for Dior, taking over the house at the age of twenty-one when Dior died. Saint Laurent attracted controversy with designs such as his 'Trapeze' dress of 1958 and his leather jackets and turtle-neck sweaters of 1960. Though hugely popular, his youthful style did not please Dior's more conventional clients – he was replaced by Marc Bohan in 1961. Following the establishment of his own house in the same year, he produced a series of innovative designs including the famous 1965 Mondrian dress, thigh-high boots, velvet knickerbockers, see-through blouses and the classic safari jacket. In 1966 Saint Laurent launched his influential 'smoking' jacket and opened a ready-to-wear chain, Rive Gauche. From 1969, when he introduced his own version of the trouser suit, Saint Laurent based many of his designs on masculine jackets and trousers.

Ungaro, Emanuel 1933–. Designer. Born Aix-en-Provence, France, to Italian parents. Ungaro trained in his parents' tailoring firm. He moved to Paris in 1955 and worked for Maison Camps tailors before joining Balenciaga in 1958. In 1962 he began working for Courrèges. Three years later Ungaro opened his own house, creating futuristic designs including angular coats, thigh-high boots and metal bras. In 1968 he launched a ready-to-wear line.

Valentino 1932–. Designer. Born Voghera, Italy. Valentino attended the Accademia Dell'Arte in Milan and the Chambre Syndicale de la Haute Couture in Paris. He worked for Dessès and Laroche in the early 1950s, before opening his own house in Rome in 1959. In 1962 Valentino transferred to Florence, where he was acclaimed for his romantic evening gowns, often with dramatic bows and ruffles. By the mid-1960s he had launched his famous trouser suits for day and evening wear. Valentino was hugely successful with his 1968 White Collection, which included mini dresses worn with lacy tights and flat shoes. His signature colour is red.

Sources for 1960s Fashion

Anderson Black, J.
and Madge Garland
A History of Fashion, 1975

Baynes, Ken
and Kate Baynes, eds.
*The Shoe Show: British Shoes
since 1790*, 1979

Byrde, Penelope
*The Male Image: Men's Fashion
in England 1300–1970*, 1979

Cardin, Pierre
*Pierre Cardin: Past, Present and
Future*, 1990

Carter, Ernestine
*The Changing World of Fashion:
1900 to the Present*, 1977

Clark, Rowena, ed. (From
The Costume Institute, The
Metropolitan Museum of Art,
New York)
Fabulous Fashion: 1907–1967,
1967

Chenoune, Farid
A History of Men's Fashion, 1993

De Courtais, Georgine
*Women's Headdress and
Hairstyles*, 1973

De la Haye, Amy, ed.
*The Cutting Edge: 50 Years of
British Fashion 1947–1997*, 1996

De Marly, Diana
*Fashion for Men: An Illustrated
History*, 1985

Ewing, Elizabeth
Fur in Dress, 1981

*Dress and Undress: A History of
Women's Underwear*, 1978

History of 20th Century Fashion,
1974

Fashion Institute of Technology,
New York
*All American: A Sportswear
Tradition*, 1985

Gallery of English Costume
Weddings, 1976

Ginsburg, Madeleine
Wedding Dress 1740–1970,
1981

The Hat: Trends and Traditions,
1990

Hall-Duncan, Nancy
*The History of Fashion
Photography*, 1979

Howell, Georgina
*In Vogue: Six Decades of
Fashion*, 1975

Jarvis, Anthea
*Brides, Wedding Clothes and
Customs 1850–1980*, 1983

Kennett, Frances
*The Collectors' Book of Twentieth
Century Fashion*, 1983

Langley-Moore, Doris
*Fashion Through Fashion Plates
1771–1970*, 1971

La Vine, W. Robert
In a Glamorous Fashion, 1981

Lee-Potter, Charlie
Sportswear in Vogue, 1984

Lynham, Ruth, ed.
*Paris Fashion: Great Designers
and Their Creations*, 1972

Martin, Richard
and Harold Koda
*Jocks and Nerds: Men's Style in
the Twentieth Century*, 1989

Mulvagh, Jane
*Vogue: History of 20th Century
Fashion*, 1988

O'Hara, Georgina
The Encyclopaedia of Fashion,
1986

Peacock, John
Costume 1066 to the 1990s,
1994

*The Chronicle of Western
Costume*, 1991

20th Century Fashion, 1993

Men's Fashion, 1996

Probert, Christina
Lingerie in Vogue since 1910,
1981

Saint Laurent, Cecil
*The History of Ladies'
Underwear*, 1968

Simon, Pedro
The Bikini, 1986

Yarwood, Doreen
*English Costume: From the
Second Century to 1967*, 1967

Magazines and Journals

Cecil Gee, Trade Journals,
1962–1965, Cecil Gee Men's
Wear, London

*Failsworth Hat and Cap
Collection, Trade Journals*,
1965–1966, Failsworth Hats
(London) Ltd.

*Femme Chic: Les Documents
officiels de la haute couture de
Paris*, Paris

Honey, London

L'Art et la mode, Paris

*L'Officiel de la couture et de la
mode de Paris*, Paris

Jardin des modes, Paris

Linea Italiana, Milan

Marie France, Paris

Queen, London

Vogue, New York

Vogue, London

Vogue, Paris

Harper's Bazaar, London

Woman's Journal, London

Vogue Pattern Book, London,
New York

*Sir, Men's International Fashion
Journal*, Amsterdam

Acknowledgments

Thanks are due to the Yale
School of Art and Design,
Wrexham, Clwyd, for the use of
their facilities.